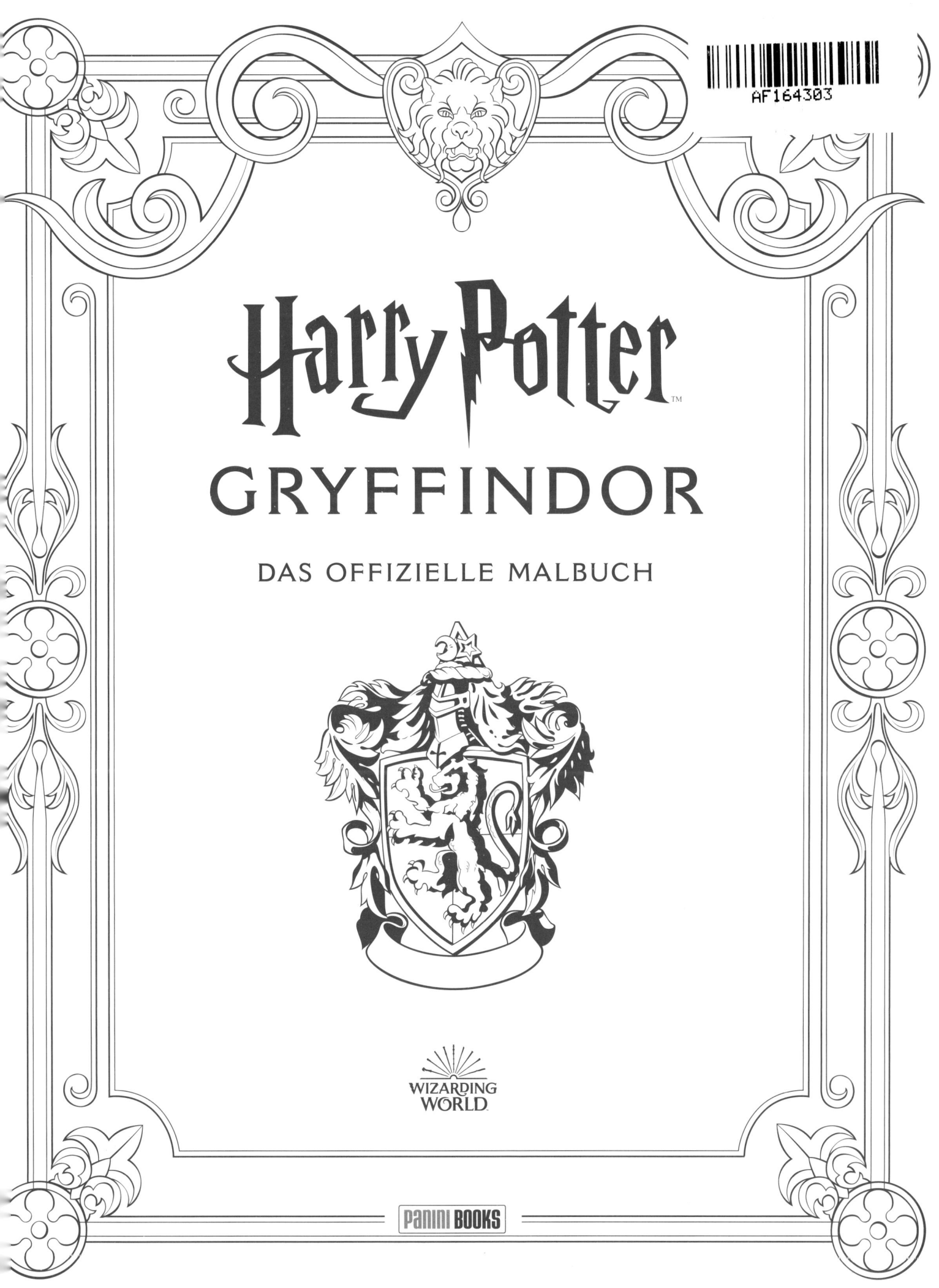

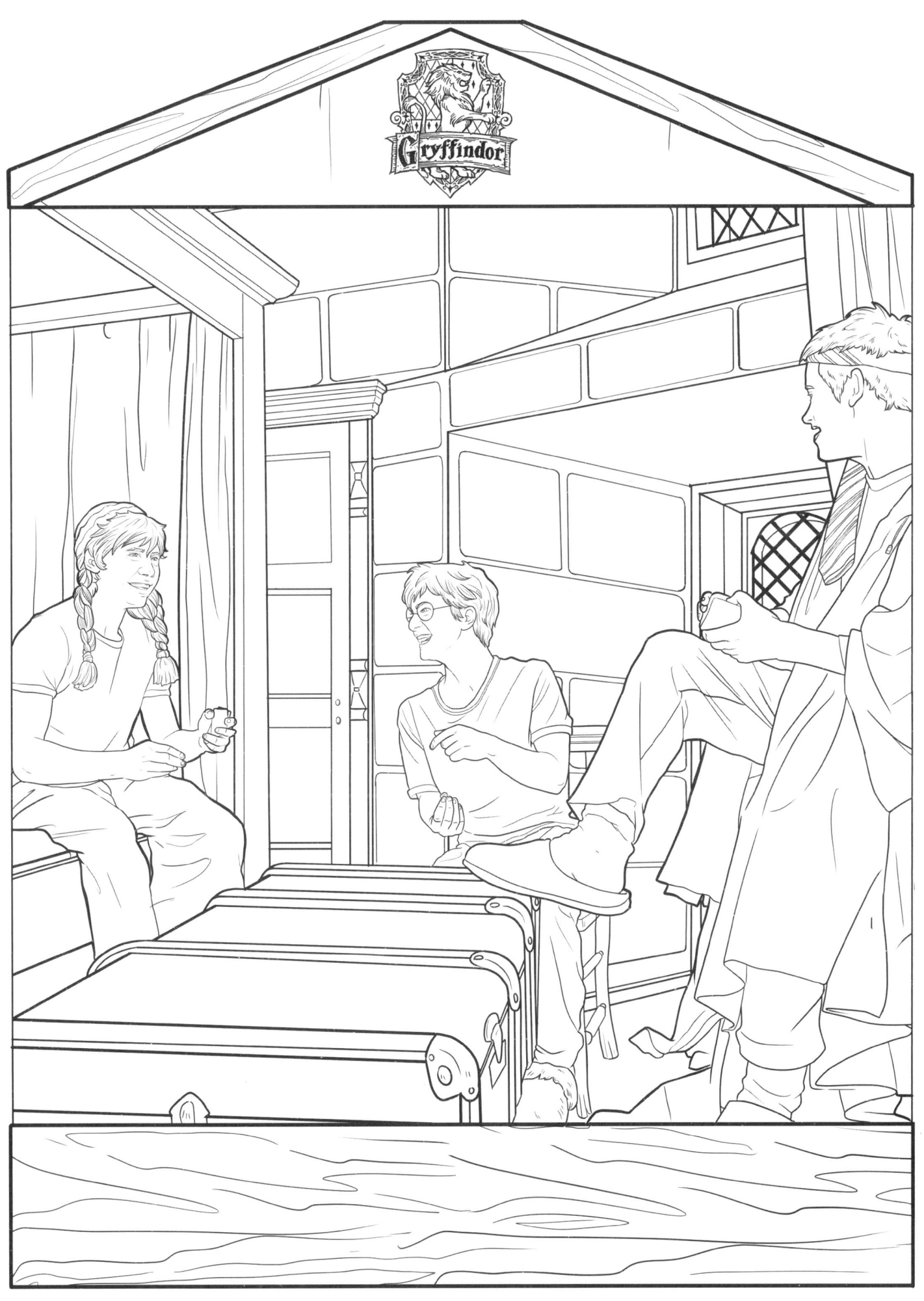

Copyright © 2021 Warner Bros. Entertainment Inc. WIZARDING WORLD characters, names and related indicia are © & ™ Warner Bros. Entertainment Inc. WB SHIELD: © & ™ WBEI. Publishing Rights © JKR. (s21)

Alle Rechte vorbehalten. Kein Teil dieser Publikation darf ohne schriftliche Genehmigung in irgendeiner Weise reproduziert werden.

3. Auflage 2025

Harry Potter – Gryffindor: Das offizielle Malbuch
Deutschsprachige Ausgabe 2021 durch die Panini Verlags GmbH,
Schloßstraße 76, 70176 Stuttgart
gpsr@panini.de
Verlagsleitung: Gabriele El Hag
Chefredaktion: Nicole Hoffart
Redaktion: Eva-Regine Rauch
Lektorat: Claudia Weber
Grafik: tab indivisuell, Stuttgart
Manufactured in China by Insight Editions
ISBN 978-3-8332-4040-9

Die Deutsche Nationalbibliothek verzeichnet diese Publikation in der Deutschen Nationalbibliografie; detaillierte bibliografische Daten sind im Internet über http://dnb.d-nb.de abrufbar.

Englische Originalausgabe 2021
Insight Editions, San Rafael, California

Publisher: Raoul Goff
VP of Licensing and Partnerships: Vanessa Lopez
VP of Creative: Chrissy Kwasnik
VP of Manufacturing: Alix Nicholaeff
Editorial Director: Vicki Jaeger
Senior Editor: Greg Solano
Design Support: Megan Sinaed-Harris and Monique Narboneta
Associate Editor: Anna Wostenberg
Senior Production Editor: Elaine Ou
Senior Production Manager: Greg Steffen
Senior Production Manager, Subsidiary Rights: Lina s Palma

Thanks to all our artists: Remie Geoffroi, Maxime LeBrun, Pablo Matamoros, Hend_draw from Fiverr, Tomato Farm, Conor Buckley, Paula Hanback, and Iván Fernández Silva